"Want to make me the happiest, healthiest, best-behaved dog in the neighborhood?

"Afraid that you don't always know how I feel, or what I want, or what's good for me?

"Well, you're in luck, because in this little book, with help from lots of my friends (and a very understanding human named Anne Bobby), I answer all of your questions—and offer lots of good advice, stories, and easy tips for making our life together better than ever.

"And check out our pictures—we're pretty cute, if I do say so myself."

photo: Suzanne Kunz

Love Me
· or ·
Leash Me

Love Me
• or •
Leash Me

● ● ● ● ● ● ● ● ● ● ● ●

50 Simple Ways to Keep Me a Happy, Healthy and Well-Behaved Companion

As Told to Anne Bobby

BLACK DOG
& LEVENTHAL
PUBLISHERS

Published by
Black Dog & Leventhal Publishers, Inc.
151 West 19th Street
New York, NY 10011

Distributed by
Workman Publishing Company
708 Broadway
New York, NY 10003

Cover and book design by Sheila Hart Design, Inc.
Sepia-toned photographs from Jim Dratfield's Petography
(www.petography.com)
Manufactured in the United States of America

ISBN: 1-57912-215-9

h g f e d c b a

Library of Congress Cataloging-in-Publication Data

Bobby, Anne.
Love me or leash me : 50 simple ways to keep me a happy, healthy and well-behaved
companion / as told to Anne Bobby.
p. cm.
ISBN 1-57912-215-9 (hardcover : alk. paper)
1. Dogs--Training 2. Dogs--Behavior. I. Title.
SF431 .B57 2001
636.7'0887--dc21
2001003644

ANNE BOBBY has appeared in dozens of films, television shows, and plays. She is an animal rescuer and a long-time volunteer at the same Brooklyn veterinary hospital where she takes her cats (yes, cats). This is her first book. • **JIM DRATFIELD** is the creative director and photographer of Petography, Inc., specializing in fine art photography of pets and their people: www.petography.com. Jim is the author of *The Quotable Canine*, *The Quotable Feline*, *Pug Shots* and the upcoming *Underdogs*. He share's his life with his black labrador, Caleb.

photo: H. Knight

This book is dedicated to Francis DiPietro,

The lost souls still searching for a home,

And those tireless individuals who will always have room in their

hearts for one more.

And, with love and fondest memories, to Prospect. My Best Girl.

I miss you.

Acknowledgments

A very special thank-you to all the dog owners and dog lovers who contributed to this book—your stories and photos were both inspirational and touching, and your dogs, a blessing. Cheers. • James Dratfield, thank you for your remarkable gift and endless patience—and thanks, Caleb, for loaning me your dad. • Thanks to Dr. Mark Gibson of Animal Kind Veterinary hospital for helping to keep my facts straight, and to the entire staff for providing such excellent care to the pets of Park Slope. • Thanks also to William Kiester, Laura Ross and Hadar Makov for all the fun. • Chris Schelling, I must be doing some good on this earth if you're in my life. Thank you for believing. • Beth Fleisher, you make sense, and you always have. Elizabeth Barrows, you care, and it shows in everything you do. Thank you both. • Thanks and love beyond measure to my family and especially Kate Bobby—my best friend, and the finest writer I know.

Foreword

I love listening to dogs. I've been listening to them for about three years now, since I started working with abandoned dogs in my Brooklyn neighborhood. I visit them in their temporary shelters several times a week and … *listen*. • They tell me what they like. • They tell me what they don't. • They tell me when they're too afraid to come close. • They tell me when they're ready to start trusting me. • They tell me they're happy to see me, and which treat is their favorite, baloney or a bully stick. • They tell me where they like to be petted. • Sometimes they tell me that I look like I've had a bad day, and they do something that helps me forget my problems. • They tell me when they're sad, or lonely, or unwell, and I do something that helps them remember how much they are loved. • Eventually, these dogs leave me. Other people see how wonderful these dogs are and adopt the dogs one by one. With a little luck, I will never see these dogs again. And that is exactly the way it should be. * Maybe it's because I want these strays to find a home so badly that I spend so much time listening to what they are saying. Every dog has a unique spirit; so long as the spirit of a dog is nurtured—so long as a dog is encouraged to speak its mind— its human counterpart will recognize his or her soul mate, and adopt the right dog for both of them. * This book is the result of my many years in cages, hospitals, shelters, and parks, in alleys, and along miles of tracking down more dogs than I'd care to admit but that I can still name, and will always love. * I am honored that these dogs have shared their experiences with me, and I am happy to serve as their translator. * Enjoy their words. I sure do.

Anne Bobby

The Keys to Success

Tip 1: With boundaries and routine, every joy is possible.

Any age, any breed, any size, there are two things we count on you to provide, as important as the food, shelter, and love you've already given:

Boundaries:

Let us know we are safe to explore, test ourselves, and learn, for you are there to protect us from harm.

Reassure us that you'll never let us eat what we shouldn't or face an obstacle that could harm us or feel that we're ever in danger.

Routine:

When we know which things in life will always be there, we grow confident, happy, and open to new things, people, and experiences.

photo: courtesy R. Cholakian

SAM is a Cairn terrier who loves to hike,
carry big sticks and even small dogs!

About Training

Tip 2: We all need training, and we <u>want</u> it, too!

In every little dog beats the heart of a wolf (and every big dog thinks he fits in a teacup —or at least in your lap). That is why, no matter what size we are, you've got to train us. Training doesn't just ensure that a Great Dane won't pull her owner's arm out of the socket. It also allows a Pomeranian to coexist happily with people and socialize well with his buddies. So make sure we're trained—it may save our lives!

photo: Tien Tran, courtesy D. Seltzer

Life on the streets may have been hard for RUFFIAN, but this Chihuahua has gone on to become an agility title-holder —thanks to training and love.

Make Walks Special

Tip 3: When walking me, talk to me.

Sometimes you guys mistake quantity time with quality time when it comes to walking us. Remember, for us, walk time is one of the best times of the day, our chance to relax and hang out with you.

photo: L. & A. Morris

Go on and tell your dog how much YOU enjoy your time together. Talk to him when you walk him. Bring a toy along, have some fun. It will give both of you something to look forward to next time. It sure works for me!

When taking her walk, Lab-mix PAX likes to jump in puddles with her mom and dad!

Dogs and Errands

Tip 4: If you <u>have</u> to duck into the store and leave me outside, leave me in charge of something.

For you, it's a quick stop at the deli—for me, it sometimes feels like the end of the world. I don't know a single one of us who likes being left outside a store. It leaves us vulnerable to strangers, and may make us act in ways we don't like. But if you have to go inside somewhere and leave me tied up nearby, leave me in charge of something of yours —

a scarf, a glove, a newspaper, or a small package you've picked up along the way. Whatever it is, it will bear your scent and can help calm me down. Watching over something of yours also makes me feel like a useful part of the team. (And MAKE SURE I am wearing tags and have an ID chip implant or tattoo ID!)

photo: S. White, M. Lapthorn

She's a long way from the Humane Society
in Vieques, Puerto Rico, but Chihuahua-mix
RAMONA has taken to her Brooklyn life
with gusto, enjoying both shopping
and socializing down at the pub with her friends.

Easy Listening

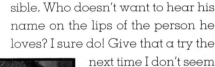

Tip 5: The more you <u>talk</u> to me, the more I'll listen.

Sometimes all it takes is the proper tone of voice. We're very sensitive, you know, and anxiety or tension in a voice can make the more, shall we say, *attuned* dog freak out a bit. Try using a special tone of voice just for speaking to me, and call me by name as much as possible. Who doesn't want to hear his name on the lips of the person he loves? I sure do! Give that a try the next time I don't seem to want to pay attention. Keep your voice light and pleased, and find a gentle, almost musical sound to lend to my name. That will be a reward all its own!

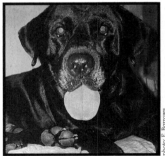

photo: E. Barrows

Former pound puppy Ambrose
is a Lab-mix who lives for his dog bed,
and his mom's lap!

4 and a Tail's Treats That Rock!

From behind the counter of 4 and a Tail, his pet supply store in Brooklyn, Sam has seen every breed of dog known to man and countless unique mixed breeds. Each dog that crosses the threshold is greeted with a dismissive toss of the head from Fluffy, the resident cat-curmudgeon, and offered a treat from Sam as a way of breaking the ice. • Sam has handed out every treat on the market, and these are some that meet with the greatest enthusiasm from pups and owners alike:

photo: courtesy 4 and a Tail

1. **Cluckers**: Pure chicken breast, diced, sliced, and dried. "These are delicious," Sam says, "and full of protein."
2. **Freeze-dried Lamb Hearts**: "The dogs go crazy for these; they're a very special treat for them."
3. **Ham-and Cheese-filled Rawhide Bone (by Red Barn)**: "They're made from compressed rawhide, which is good, and the filling takes a while for them to get out—they work for it." (He also recommends Red Barn's Filled Bones).
4. **Freeze-dried Lamb Sausage Links (Merrick)**: "These? They're gone in two bites."
5. **Greenies**: Bone-shaped chew treats, made with your dog's oral hygiene in mind—not only do they taste great, they clean your dog's teeth and freshen his breath. "These are amazing—expensive, but worth it. They're good for the dogs, too—excellent." (They have a web site—go to www.kissablepets.com for details.)
6. **Bully Sticks**: "Of course, bully sticks. Every dogs tries to get one of them out of the box." (Never heard of them? See tip #15!)
7. **Dog Biscuits (5 flavors, from Mother Hubbard)**: "They're good for the bigger dogs, excellent for their teeth." (For smaller dogs, Mother Hubbard also makes filled Marrow Bone Treats.)
8. **Freeze-dried Beef Liver Treats (Pro-Treat)**: "The best thing for when you're training your dog." (Pro-Treat also sells Freeze-dried Chicken.)
9. **Beef Chips**: "Pure beef—they love that!"
10. **Anything you're eating**: "That's what they *really* want!

Straight from the "Hearts and Homes": Mel Salamone and Roseann Savasta

It's a familiar sight in Brooklyn —a brightly painted pickup truck full of tools and pups, parked near the courthouse. Outside on the sidewalk are more dogs, a gentle but scarred Pit Bull asleep on a blanket, two rambunctious Husky mixes chewing on donated toys, one elderly moppet of a mix quietly munching on lunch. People stop by and give donations, dropping change and bills into a plastic jug guarded by a sweetheart of a Chihuahua who will give a kiss at no charge.

• It's just another day at "Hearts and Homes for Homeless Dogs," a grass-roots rescue and adoption organization run by Mel Salamone, Roseann Savasta, and a team of remarkable volunteers. For over ten years, Mel and Roseann have been doing their part to defend the stray and abused dogs in their community, taking in the dogs, tending their wounds, boarding them and finding them homes—for many, the first one of their lives. The heartache is intense—as is the financial strain—but Mel and Roseann remain passionate about their cause. • As they enter their second decade of dog rescue, their passions have extended beyond the care of the dogs. Now Mel and Roseann are addressing animal cruelty directly. Within weeks of each other, two dogs find their way into Mel's rescue van, which doubles as a truck for his scrap-metal business. One mutt is found by the Brooklyn docks, starving to death. His broken leg has left him unable to look for food. The second dog, a Pit Bull, has been tied up with wire and abused beyond description. • "These are not just homeless dogs," says Anthony Salamone, Mel's brother and a volunteer with the organization. "There are beautiful living creatures suffering out there. People need to know. We can't turn away from them anymore and pretend abuse isn't happening." • With advocates like "Hearts and Homes," and with the support of the community, the message is getting out—and lives are being saved.

There are local animal rescue groups in your neighborhood in need of help. Seek these organizations out. Offer them the gift of your time, your financial support, donations of food, blankets, toys, or simply a sympathetic ear. Adopt a stray from these heroes, or foster a puppy or dog for them. Space can be scarce!

"Hearts and Homes" has a web site: They are listed, along with organizations nationwide, at www.petfinder.com—visit today!

Poop Eating

Tip 6: If I eat my poop, I may need a change in my diet.

First things first—many of us eat poops. And yes, it's pretty gross. But it may also mean that we are lacking digestive enzymes and need our diet to be supplemented with enzyme-containing foods like pumpkin (seed it if your dog is small!) or pineapple. Mixing meat tenderizers into our food is another way of getting us to stop eating our poop. I've got to be honest, though, none of these things seem to stop us from eating somebody else's. It's just one of those things. I mean, come on, you'll never explain what's so great about coffee, we can't explain the thing with poop!

photo: J. Martineau

After surviving being thrown from a car, Chihuahua TWELVE figures she can pretty much eat whatever she wants!

Well, it tastes
good to me...

To Neuter or Not to Neuter

Tip 7: Neutering can add years to my life — and ease my stress!

You probably know that intact males are more likely to fight because of the effect of testosterone on their behavior. But an intact dog can actually become a victim of neutered dogs, who can become threatened by the scent of testosterone.

photo: courtesy D. Solomon

• Intact dogs also run a higher risk of getting prostate infections and testicular cancer. And let's just say the number of un-neutered dogs that run away in search of some "satisfaction," is cause enough for me to speak out in favor of neutering your male dog!

TESSA is a Spinone Italiano who loves to chew the ears of her boyfriend, Golden Retriever Quincy—who happens to be neutered.

My Bed

Tip 8: If you want to keep me off the furniture, be sure I have a special place of my own to hang out on.

Crates aren't just for travel, you know—after all, who doesn't need a little privacy now and then? • If you don't want me to treat your furniture like my personal boudoir, set up my crate and show me that I have a room of my own. I'll feel important, and it's a great way of helping me adjust to the fact that there are some places in the house that are just yours. • (The crate is also a helpful solution for those of us who get all stressed out at bedtime. Just keep it near your bed, throw in a few toys and a blanket—and leave the door open!)

photo: courtesy D. Gillman

Border Collie-mix OSO is a contemplative "philosopher-dog" with a favorite place to lay his head —the sunniest patch of the porch.

Good Dog!

Tip 9: A treat secret from the pros.

What tiny treat do the best dog handlers use to get us to pose at dog shows? • What nutritious tidbit is high in protein and extremely tasty to us? • What inexpensive morsel can be crushed up and sprinkled over our food when we're feeling finicky? • What treat will we do ANYTHING for? • **Freeze-dried Beef Liver**, available at any pet store. (And, by the way, cats love it, too!)

photo: D. Savatteri

Watch out when you tell TASHA to "sit."
This 90-pound Giant Schnauzer will probably sit on
your foot and, if there's a liver treat involved,
she won't move until you've given her more!

Protect Me from the Sun

Tip 10: You're wearing sunscreen. I need it, too.

Middle of summer? We're going for a picnic? Great! How about you spread a little of that sunblock around? Sure, we get sunburned, too — especially light-col-ored and shorthaired dogs. Protect me from the harmful rays by applying a little sunblock around my nose and ears. Be sure to rub it though, because I might try to make a snack of it.

photo: J. Beaver

Chocolate Lab FANNIE knows that summer
is the best time to swim across her favorite lake
—a mile wide!

Living With Dogs:
Positive Reinforcement

Through their absolute understanding of and respect for the species, Polly Hanson and Bud Greenberg have brought out the best in neglected, abused, and misunderstood dogs for over fifteen years—turning some into caregivers in their own right, and changing the

photos: courtesy P. Hanson, B. Greenberg

way all of them are regarded by society. • The "training," Polly says, she leaves for the owners. • "Dogs are genetically equipped to do behaviors," she explains. "We can't get dogs to unlearn these things. What I teach them is *when* they are allowed to do these behaviors."

• Lexie is a beautiful Terrier-mix who has come under Polly's tutelage with an extremely aggressive streak. Armed with a bag of chopped-up chicken, Polly takes Lexie on a walk with her latest owners (she's had four previous homes). They are accompanied by nine-year-old Chow-mix, Little Bear, one of the dogs that live with Polly and Bud full-time. As they walk, Polly gives both dogs pieces of chicken—even when Lexie barks, postures, and snaps at Little Bear. • Some trainers might suggest that this is the time to say, "No!" or "Bad dog!" and deprive the dog of a reward. But Polly says nothing, just lets Lexie bark. Then when Lexie is quiet and her body language indicates a lack of aggression, Polly reaches out and gives her more chicken. • "What would a reprimand and punishment teach this dog about snapping?" Polly

asks. "The dogs would just feel more scared the next time, if she had been 'shorted out' for following her hard-wired instincts." • But not reprimanding is only part of the lesson for the day. Instead of simply depriving Lexie for snapping and barking, Polly gives Lexie more chicken the next time the dog *doesn't* bark and snap. Lexie neither barks nor snaps for the rest of her walk—the first time, her owners say, that Lexie has walked with another dog without displaying aggressive behavior toward it. • Polly suggests to owners Jim and Jane that they should purchase training "clickers" to indicate to Lexie which specific behaviors they like, the ones for which she's getting the praise and treats. • "With this kind of positive reinforcement, Lexie has just learned that she will get a reward when she appears relaxed around other dogs," Polly explains. "Soon we will be able to build on this accomplish-ment. Lexie's doing very well." • ("It's like a switch flipped," Jim says a few weeks into Polly's training. "We take Lexie to the park now, and she has friends she actually *plays* with. She's a different girl— it's a miracle!")

photos: courtesy P. Hanson, B. Greenberg

Save That Stray: Adopting a Shelter Dog

The stray dog population in America has filled the shelters with more dogs than anyone can know. Taking in one of these animals is both a kindness and a reward, for these dogs are as needy and capable of receiving and giving love as any dog that has always known a home and loving owner. • A shelter, however, can be a traumatic place for those looking to adopt a stray—the sight of dozens, sometimes hundreds of abandoned animals is heartbreaking. DON'T LET THAT STOP YOU. Simply prepare yourself for the experience. Your reward is on the other side of that door. • If you're planning on going to your local pound or shelter to adopt a dog, don't go alone. Bring along a friend, a neighbor, or family member who can help you choose just the right dog. • Don't forget you can't save all of them, you can't take every dog home. Even the saddest, most lost dog has the right to choose his owner. Many of the dogs in shelters today are there because someone took them in recklessly, without consideration for what that dog's needs would be. Keep your heart in place and choose the dog that speaks to you. Look for that dog—he's there, waiting for you. • If you don't find him or her right away, or can't decide, go outside. Take a walk. *Think* about

photo: Scott Citron

your decision. Reflect on which dog is leaving the biggest impression on you. Consider what that dog's special needs might be, and whether you are capable of meeting those needs. The MOST important thing is that this dog never be displaced again. • You have to think about the health of the animal. If you're considering a dog that shows signs of injury, understand that that dog may require more care than you are able to provide. If the dog has visible scars, she may have been abused, and will need a great deal of patience. As with

JEB is a brave Terrier-mix
whose only fear is a strong wind (it hurts his ears!)

any healthy dog, your dog will require training, and it is critical that you understand the responsibilities you are taking on. Saving a dog today isn't enough. By bringing him home, you are taking charge of his well-being for the rest of his life. • You can do it. • Bring a friend. • Accept that you cannot save them all. • Remember that your dog is in there, looking for you. Let your dog choose you. • And don't forget that your dog may require specific care. • Make a reasoned decision, not an emotional one, when you take home a stray. • And enjoy your life together!

Time Out for "Time Out"

Tip 11: If you don't catch me "in the act," don't try and discipline me later.

I know it's tough, but the only time you should reprimand me for any behavior you don't like is THE MOMENT I've done it. After that, I have no idea what it is you're unhappy about. I won't understand why you're saying, "naughty girl" — I may think it's because I just gave you a kiss or something. Now you don't want me to stop *that*, do you?

photo: J.P. Leventhal

If only MAGGIE didn't look so cute
after making a snack of her dad's glasses...

Same Old Meal—Perfect!

Tip 12: We are sensitive to changes in our kibble —don't disrupt our routine too much.

When it comes to store-bought dry and wet foods, changing my diet can result in diarrhea, unless you get me used to the new food gradually by mixing it in with my old food. So try not to mess with a good thing more often than you have to. I'll thank you for that boring breakfast every morning! • (That's not to say I don't like my food supplemented by some new things —see Tip #44 for more info, and add some freshly prepared food to my mix. Nothing is better for us!)

photo: A. Wallach

SCOOTER is always at the head of the table, especially on steak night.

Excuse me...
but I don't think
I ordered this.

Dogs and Play

Tip 13: Dog play can look rough —watch my body language.

Fact one: Dogs *love* to play with each other. • Fact two: Dogs at play resemble dogs at war. • That doesn't mean we need to be separated, and that doesn't mean you should interfere. • Watch our body language when we play—are our tails wagging? Are we trading off on submissive and playful postures (rolling on our sides, arching our front paws and chests to the ground)? Are we nipping at one another's ears and tails, and NOT at eyes and back legs? • We'll let you know if we've had enough. Watch us for bristled fur, fangs, and staring with lunging, instead of

submissive postures and retreating. Listen for growling and persistent, urgent barking. • Honestly, if all you see and hear is a lot of jumping and hitting the deck, we're probably just having a good time. • Cross my heart!

photo: H. Knight, R. & I. Froburn

GINGER (l.) and APPLE (r.) are
a Pit-mix and Staffordshire Terrier
who may look scary when they play,
but the truth is they are
inseparable best friends.

A Calming Element

Tip 14: We get anxious, too!

Just like you, I sometimes feel nervous or anxious. • Well, have you ever heard of "Rescue Remedy"? • It's a great homeopathic solution made of plant essences, designed to help with anxiety. It was created a long time ago for people, but veterinarians have been using it on cats and dogs for years! Just put a drop on my nose for me to lick off, or on my food, and help me deal with all of life's little worries!

photo: K. Michel, B. Vye

When Shepherd-mix MINGUS isn't dancing or swimming, you can usually find him shelling his own pistachios.

No worries here!

Good Dog!

Tip 15: As a special treat, give me a bully stick.

Brace yourself. You may not like this, but I sure do. • Once a week or so—as often as you might have a sundae or a cigar—try giving your best friend a bully stick. You don't want to know what it is (okay, it's a dried bull penis), but we LOVE them. They're softer than rawhides and break down in our stomachs, so they won't harm us (unless you give us too many, then we get the runs). They're also full of protein, and they taste good and, you know what? They're our favorite!

photo: L. Willard

Norwich Terrier BUDDY will do anything
his dad says, before he says it,
when there's a bully stick at stake!

Bully for me!

There's Something About Gort: Griffin Dunne

Actor. Director. Producer. Manhattan-based buddy of Gort, the Norwich Terrier who very nearly stole the screen from Cameron Diaz in the Farrelly Brother's smash hit, There's Something About Mary. Charlie Wessler, the film's producer, was so taken with Gort during the shoot that when the film wrapped, he took the dog home. Now, when Wessler's film schedule gets wild, he drops the renowned pup off for a visit to the Big Apple with his pal, Griffin.

"Gort loves New York, nothing about this city phases him,"

Griffin says of his house-guest. "Except, oddly enough, the dog parks.' • "It's embarrassing, really, but Gort just doesn't seem to acknowledge that he's a dog. He doesn't want to play with other dog, or sniff their privates, he just sort of runs off in horror. See, I think he's convinced he's one of us. He just figures he's got more hair and two more legs than everybody else." • Sadly, the two have yet to collaborate artistically. Dunne certainly has nothing but praise and respect for Gort's ease in front of the camera, and his ability to improvise. • "Gort is an impulsive, almost obsessive, licker. If he gets close to your face he just licks and licks. But he uses it, really goes with his instincts. That scene in 'Mary' where he licks that woman's mouth?... All his. It was all his idea. He's great, a great actor." • Amazing, when one considers that Gort was only about six months old when he made his auspicious film debut. ("He was born looking very old.") Clearly, this dog has years of great work ahead of him. • "I'd love to work with him myself," Dunne says, although he concedes that as with their human counterparts, great animal stars come at a hefty asking price, and narrow windows of availability. "It's been a dry year for my production company when it comes to the really great canines." • Of course it's hard to hold a grudge when it comes to Gort, and the two buddies remain close. There is, however, one sticking point in their friendship. • "Charlie's a pilot, and when they fly together, Gort just gets up front, curls up, and listens to his music." Dunne pauses. "Gort likes that guy. The one with the hair, and the sound, that — Yanni. That's him. He listens to Yanni."

The Biggest Heart: Prospect
Part One – Rescue

I knew her for less than a year, but she will live in my heart forever. She showed me how much a heart can freely give of itself. She proved to everyone who met her that gratitude, trust, and love are attributes not exclusive to the human race. • It was a beautiful April morning. I was on my way to work, walking to the subway, when I caught sight of a skinny little Pit Bull walking alone on the next block. She wasn't hurt, but I knew she could become injured, oblivious as she was to the cars that slowed for her as she wandered across the street and into Prospect Park. • I saw a policeman standing on a corner nearby and ran over to him. "Can you help me catch her?" I asked, pointing to the dog. • It was unfair of me, I knew, but I had to ask. "Sorry." I followed the dog into a small playground off the park entrance, where she sat herself down to watch the children play. Thin as she was—and she was *thin*—I couldn't get over how pretty she looked, her coat the color of milky coffee, her brown eyes wide and kind. She had a small series of wrinkles across her brow that gave her a sweet look, and I guessed she had some

photo: courtesy E. Barrows

Sharpei in her genes a few generations back. • I sat down on the ground beside her. She didn't move away, instead sniffing my leg. Slowly I reached over and stroked her flank, wincing as I felt her bones. She had a collar around her neck with a phone number, and I dialed it. • "Car service." • "Yes, hi, do you have a Pit Bull?"

• "A Pit? Yeah, we've got a dog." • "Okay, well, she's here in Prospect Park." • "Oh…No, that's not our dog." • "But your number's here on her collar." • "I don't know what to tell you, that's not our dog." • It occurred to me that I was going to be very late for work. "Listen," I said, "can you just tell me what her name is?" • "Her name?" • "What's her name?" I felt my voice tightening as my anger rose. "She'll listen to me better if I call her by her name." • "She don't got no name." • I couldn't resist. "I thought you said she wasn't your dog." • *Click.* • I had let go of her collar, but the dog hadn't moved. She just sat there, looking at me as if to say, *"I could have told you they weren't interested in me. Why do you think I left?"* Right there, I named her Prospect. She had a name now. • As I looped the detachable shoulder strap of my purse around her neck, I marveled at how relaxed and well behaved she seemed to be on a leash, and figured that she had probably been a taxi company's dog who had never known a life beyond a five-foot lead. As we walked together, I quickly realized that she was more malnourished than I first thought, and after a few blocks I had to carry her. • As I headed toward my veterinarian's clinic, I passed the cop in his car; he pulled over. "That dog okay?" he asked, unrolling his window. • "I guess," I huffed, shifting Prospect in my arms. "You don't know anyone who wants a dog, do you?" • The cop shook his head. "Anyway, it looks like she wants you." • I looked down at Prospect, and I knew the cop was right.

Is There a Doctor in Your House?

Tip 16: Watch me for symptoms, and know when it's time to call my doctor.

No one ever said you should take me to the vet every time we get a hangnail. But if we're showing signs of illness that you can't pinpoint, please don't try to practice first aid on us! Call or take your dog to the vet if:

- Your dog has been limping for more than 24 hours.

- Your dog has been bitten. (Many people wait too long on this one!)
- Your dog has had diarrhea for more than 72 hours, with no other symptoms.
- Your dog has bloody diarrhea and is vomiting.
- Your dog has diarrhea accompanied by loss of appetite and vomiting.
- Your dog is bleeding.

I'm feeling _much_ better,
thank you.

- Your dog is having difficulty breathing.
- There is any sign of diarrhea or vomiting accompanied by fever.
- You've noticed any change in your dog's appearance or demeanor, and have any doubts about his health.

Don't hesitate ... call that VET! He won't hold it against you for being concerned, believe me.

photo: M. Maberry

Former junkyard dog RACE
was hit by a car and left to die.
Then he was rescued.
The accident may have cost
the Shepherd-mix his right back leg,
but he got a loving home in exchange.

The Power of Eye Contact in Action — a Game

Tip 17: Making eye contact can become a great game!

To me, eye contact is like a challenge, and I try to avoid looking at another dog in the eyes for too long. There's a *great* game that shows you how to use that to my advantage! It's fun for puppies and shy dogs, and it's an easy way to coax older and, shall we say *less svelte* dogs into

Wow—
this is better than
Pilates, huh?

getting off their behinds. • Start walking around and calling, "Where's Sheba? Sheba, where'd you go?" When Sheba comes running, don't make eye contact. Just keep calling, "Sheba! Sheba!" and Sheba will start to follow you and jump and spin for you, trying to catch your eye.

photo: A. Kato-Culp

ELSA has a game of her own.
Every time her mom opens the blinds,
this Shepherd-mix spins around and around,
howling with joy!

Dogs and Dairy

Tip 18: Did you know? I'm lactose intolerant!

Some of us lack the enzyme that breaks down dairy products. I won't go into tremendous detail here, but sometimes feeding guys like me milk or milk products can lead to some embar-rassing moments. You'll know *your* dog is lactose intolerant by watching out for diarrhea. • And don't let me have that milk shake — no matter how much I say I've earned it!

photo: J. Fields

NICKY is a poodle with brains AND beauty — he's an agility champion!

Milk and cookies, please—
and hold the milk.

Hey, Baby!

Tip 19: You can help me learn that a new baby is a precious part of my family.

Bringing home a new baby? Here's a great way to help with an introduction. (Get ready. It's a two-person operation.) • Have Mom come in first. Give us a chance to say hi—it's been a while, after all, and she has this interesting, different, new-person smell all over her. Let us go into the yard together (if you have one) for some extended greeting and play, or maybe we can take a nice walk. • While we're out, here's your job, Dad: start scattering the baby's things around the house. The blankets, the car seat, the burpy-cloth (Wow, those would make a great toy. Better keep a count of them to start.). They all carry the baby's scent, and make

I really don't mind ol'
"what's her name",
not as long as I'm still
your baby, too!

me feel like he's already part of the family and house I love and protect. • You can also wrap the baby in something that smells like you, a blanket you've slept in or a T-shirt you've worn. That way, when we finally do meet, this new little person will already smell like an old friend.

photo: K. O'Brien

Shepherd-mix MAGRITTE
took no time to fall in love
with her best buddy, Garreth,
and even less time with his sister, Collette!

Getting Along: New Pets

Tip 20: I was here first. It's important that I know I haven't been replaced in your heart.

When you bring home a new dog or cat, let *me* come around to accepting him first. Give him hugs in private, when I'm not around to see. Your support during my period of adjustment will remind me that having a new face in the family doesn't mean you love me less. Whenever there's a new arrival—

Just so long as she knows that I get the first choice of laps, and the first piece of bacon that falls to the floor is mine, and nobody gets the back seat but me and oh yeah, if she thinks she can take her pick of any pillow she wants she's got another thing coming...

whether it's a cute kitten or a guy
who smells like formula—you need
to spend a lot of quality time with
me. You'd be surprised how inse-
cure some of us can be (I know,
I know, your dog is more of the
Clint Eastwood type)!

photo: D. Cody, S. LaManna

Dachshunds LUCY and ETHEL
have always gotten along —
Ethel was born with one ear, honest.

Stocking Up: The First Aid Kit

I'm not saying we need a whole shelf in the medicine cabinet, but there are a few thing that every dog-owner should definitely have on hand at all times, so that your vet or the National Animal Poison Center can better assist you in an emergency:

You're gonna stick that where?

photo: J. Dratfield – Petography

1. Mineral oil (as a laxative)
2. Tweezers
3. Gauze pads, tape and a roll of gauze or bandaging
4. Cotton balls (NOT synthetic cosmetic puffs, but PURE COTTON, for certain obstructions)
5. Hydrogen peroxide (to induce vomiting)
6. Betadine
7. A tube of antibacterial cream
8. A rectal thermometer
9. Any other medications prescribed by your vet, and the telephone numbers of your veterinarian and the Animal Poison Control Center (in case I'm in someone else's care at the time of the emergency)
10. A book of first aid for dogs.

Take a moment and make sure that you have these things in your house, and that they are readily available—and always make sure that any dog-walker or dog-sitter knows where these things are. They could help save my life someday!

Pettiquette: The Dog Run

(courtesy of Beau)

photo: courtesy G. Burrow

"So your dog wants to get out and mingle — great! For us urban dogs, socializing is very often done at "dog runs"—special areas in parks, or makeshift grounds that have been given over to dogs and their owners for exercise and play. Even country dogs enjoy getting together with their buddies for a little bit of supervised 'touch tail'!' • "It's a privilege to have a socializing space in your neighborhood, and there are some simple ways to make visiting any dog run a pleasant experience for all!"

Old-timer BEAU lives in Brooklyn and is the self-proclaimed "center of the universe."

1. When to say "wait":

"Be responsible about your dog's social aptitude. I'll go anywhere you take me, you know. It's up to you to decide whether or not I'm capable of playing well in a group. Some dogs are 'solo artists', you know. Don't try and change them, and don't try to force them onto a situation that will make fellow pups uncomfortable."

2. Keep it clean:

"Okay, even if you and I are the only ones there … c'mon, use the plastic bag. And take turns with the other 'parents' with a rake every now and then — that will make us all happy, and help keep us from making a snack of something we shouldn't." (Have you considered setting up a little 'cleaning corner' at your run?)"

3. If it's there, it's everybody's:

"If I've got some special toy that I can't live without, maybe it would be better if we left it home. I mean, heck, I can make a toy of just about anything. I'd rather you bring something I wouldn't mind the other guys taking off with. We're all pretty democratic—*most* of the time."

4. Different dog, different rules:

"Know what kind of social situation works best for me. If your dog is new, bring him to the run at a less crowded time at first, and watch him for signs of stress. Arrange 'play dates' with dogs that make a favorable impression, and likewise be mindful of situations that make him uneasy."

5. Include the outsider:

"If you see a dog having difficulty to the group, try not to exclude either the dog or the owner. If the dog is the same size as me, maybe we can hang out another time, when the run is less crowded. Don't let some poor owner think he's a failure just because his dog doesn't have the greatest social skills—the dog could end up paying a hefty price."

6. It's a free-for-all:

"If that Pug has a choice of sitting with his tennis ball or running with the Bulldogs (and Shepherds and Mastiffs), guess where he's probably gonna want to be? That's the great thing about a dog run—EVERYBODY'S a quarterback, no matter what your size. That's how dogs play, so don't bring the Poodle if you're worried about her ending up in a scrimmage. She probably will. Organize a small-dog play date at the run, if you want your Shi-Tzu to pick on someone his own size!"

7. Watch:

"Yes, you! You think I don't care if you saw me get the stick from the Basset Hound who tackled me last week? I CARE—so put down that phone, stop flirting and WATCH ME BE A HERO!"

Tennis Balls—Foul!

Tip 21: Make sure the ball I'm catching is safe.

s that a tennis ball I see? Away with it! Yeah, I know—I used to like them too. Then my dad heard about how tennis balls are made of sand, and how they can grind my teeth down. Tricky, huh? I mean, they even sell them in great doggie flavors. But no—if you're going to throw me a ball, make sure it's one that's safe for me. We really like those high bouncy blue rubber balls (just make sure you get the right size— your pet store owner will help).

photo: J. Greenwald

Bullmastiff/Pit-mix LEO is a big fan of Kooshy Balls— and hanging out with his buddies at his local bagel shop.

Dogs and Diet: Fruit

Tip 22: Some kinds of fruit can send me to the hospital.

You kidding? I love fruit! Trouble is, some fruit doesn't love me. Did you know that many big dogs end up needing surgery because they've swallowed peach and mango pits? Did you know that apple seeds contain cyanide in an amount that could be fatal to a small dog?

photo: Anne Burns

Did you know that some people believe grapes and raisins are toxic for pups? • Fruit can and should be a wonderful dietary supplement (coconut, for example is a great source of vitamins), but please be careful about keeping that fruit bowl out of my reach. I'll thank you for it!

HENRY takes his diet seriously — he spits out anything he doesn't like, including some fruit!

Time for Touch

Tip 23: Don't laugh—everyone loves a massage.

It's a wonderful feeling, getting my ears rubbed. And my shoulders—gosh, have you any idea how much weight I'm carrying around? And my toes, they're all tense from grabbing at the ground and digging in, to jump into the air and sneak a bite of whatever you're eating. Spend a little time getting to know which part of *your* dog's body needs some kneading, and give that buddy of yours a rubdown whenever you can.

photo: M. Harrison, H. Scarbrough

When she isn't off hunting squirrels, Greyhound-mix ZORA is probably looking to get her belly rubbed.

For the Bored

Tip 24: Give us a project and watch us go!

This is a great game for the big-time chewer: Take a favorite smelly treat (liver treats are great for this, or a little piece of salami). Find a rag and knot the treat inside. Make as many knots as you can, and then give it to me. Watch how many hours I spend working that one out!

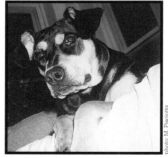

photo: M. Pisciotta

There's no end to potential treats for Shepherd-mix ELLA —mom and dad own a restaurant!

Was that—
a liver treat?

Don't Wander Off

Tip 25: Keep me on the leash for regular walks.

When it comes to leashes and walks, we may disagree. I know you don't want me to feel "restricted," that you think a leash curtails my freedom on my walk. But trust me, I don't see my leash as a torture implement. My leash is my way of keeping track of you.

photo: C. Claremont, B. Fleisher

When you take my leash away, I have to keep making sure that you haven't run off or gotten in trouble. Don't worry, I'll feel "free" when we get to the park. When we're out just walking, let's stay connected. It helps me show the rest of the world that we belong to each other.

Collie-mix PADRAIC was found trying to sneak into his local Saint Patrick's Day parade. Now he watches from the sidewalk—with his family.

Love Song: Michael Cerveris & Gibson

photo: C. Hatherly

He's performed all over the world in such cutting-edge musicals as Titanic, *The Who's Tommy* and Hedwig and the Angry Inch. *He juggles his theatrical appearances with a busy film and television career, as well as performing with fellow musicians on stage and in the recording studio. Clearly, actor-singer-songwriter*

Michael Cerveris is a very busy guy. But this hard-working, hard-rocking performer has a soft spot for a very special girl in his life — a beautiful, Border Collie-mix named Gibson. Writing from London, where he was filming a television show, Michael had this to say about his beloved dog.

"As a puppy, when she came home with me from the Manhattan ASPCA, Gibson showed a keen interest in the guitars lying around my apartment. A little too keen, I was afraid, and I put them in the cases that still bear her needle-sharp tooth marks. But it did seem only natural that she should be named after the instruments in which we shared such an interest. • "Even before she had the shots she needed to brave the streets of New York City, Gibson attended my band's Gig's at Sin E, an East Village venue, cradled in my girlfriend's arms. She was often more popular than the band, accepting the adoration of those around her with a quizzical expression and a royal demeanor. • "She's never really expressed a great interest in any one particular style of music, though she seems to prefer my playing acoustic guitar to electric. She not much of a singer herself, and drums are not big on her list of favorite things. But over the years she has accompanied me almost everywhere. She even appeared onstage once (by invitation), at the final curtain call of the closing night of *Tommy* in Germany. • "I did worry a bit initially that seeing me in a variety of costumes and wigs might be disturbing or at least confusing for her, but neither my Mod bowl cut nor seeing me in full drag seems to ruffle her fur. When I walked into the first costume run-through of *Hedwig and the Angry Inch* with boots, pink-fringed mini-dress, and several feet of bleached Farrah curls, Gibson just gave me an "Oh, *Dad...*" sort of look and sat back down under her seat. • "'Under her seat' is the way most people who know her probably think of Gibson. She will almost always look for a chair, table, or amp case with the lowest possible clearance under which to squeeze while she patiently waits until I'm done doing whatever useless bit of performing (or in the case of auditions, groveling) I need to do before we can go home again.

• "Through the kindness and indulgence of many directors, managers, staff and co-workers, Gibson has accompanied me to rehearsals and performances throughout our years together. For the most part, she is a model of decorum and is perfectly relaxed and quiet, except on those rare occasions when she thinks someone is acting badly (or badly acting). She gets nervous only when she doesn't know where I am. But she does have the neurotic disposition of most great artists and makes people work for her attention and affection. I've often returned to a dressing room at intermission to find crew members or actors lying prone on the floor with a bit of cookie in an outstretched hand pleading softly for her to come out and play. Such persistence usually pays off, and I think people are sadder to see her go than me when a show ends. • "Most fascinating is how quickly she learns my routine. She figures out when I'm coming into the dressing room to change. At intermission, she'll get up and stretch, have a little water, nose around her toys and stick her nose in the hallway to see what all the other silly humans are doing. At the end of the night she waits until all my makeup is off before she starts to get excited for the walk or occasional cab ride home. • "She's a show-biz dog, but is gracefully unaffected by all the fuss and hoopla. Rock club or recording studio, Broadway palace, or regional dive, Gibson takes it all in stride. She's been across the country and all over Europe (with the exception of Britain, because of their cruel and archaic quarantine laws which still exclude vaccinated and healthy North American animals), and she treats everyone from ushers to stars with the same equanimity. In fact, she tends to give big shots more of a hard time, and she seems particularly distrustful of directors and producers. THAT, I think she gets from me."

The Curious Dog

Tip 26: Your dog is your child, and will do childish things.

Not all dogs are a smart as I am. I know the difference between my toys and yours (well, there's the time I chewed up the contents of your gym bag, but that was because you were spending too much time away from home). But some dogs just can't stop thinking that what's *yours* is *theirs*. • Don't make it harder for the curious dog: Puppy-proof your home, and treat her as you'd treat a baby—because that's what she is! Give her lots of toys of her own to play with, reward her with a treat and praise when she does what you ask, and try not to get too angry when she's made an honest

I always remember not to do this.
I just always remember
a little too late.

mistake. • (Of course that doesn't mean a little discipline isn't sometimes called for — boundaries, remember? And if this is the third time she's stuck her head in that fish, I think we're looking at a *serious* "time out.")

photo: B. Gidella

Despite her fondness for
"perfectly good chicken carcasses"
when she was a puppy, no one ever sent
Newfoundland ABBY packing!

On the Road

Tip 27: Plan our car trips safely.

Don't let me guilt you out. The car is for trips when you know I will *never* be left inside unattended. Even a few minutes in an overheated car can cost me my life. Or I might ingest something I shouldn't, succumb to hypothermia or break a window if I become alarmed. And while you may like the idea of having your best buddy sitting next to you admiring how you obey the rules of the road, I belong in my crate—for my own sake.

photo: D. Seltzer

SPUD loves to be indoors, even in hotel rooms
—so long as his mom is with him
and there's a French fry to be found!

Chocolate: Myths and Facts

Tip 28: While the amount of toxicity varies, avoid giving me any chocolate.

O kay, everyone's heard how "dogs are allergic to chocolate," that even a little bit of the stuff is dangerous to us. But *why* is it? • Here's the deal. It's the caffeine in the chocolate, as well as the theobromine (the main alkaloid of the cacao bean) that causes seizures in dogs. There's no fixed amount of chocolate that causes harm—it all depends on my size and the amount of caffeine and theobromine I ingest. • So which chocolate contains the most caffeine and theobromine? The general rule is: the darker the chocolate, the higher the caffeine content. One 1-ounce bar of Hershey's dark chocolate contains three times as much as its milk chocolate counterpart;

and unsweetened baking chocolate, *ten times* the caffeine—but, really, giving me *any* kind of chocolate is unhealthy. Face it: Chocolate is fattening, it's bad for my teeth, and if it's got a lot of caffeine and theobromine, it could prove fatal. • There you go— all you need to know. Now next time I'm trying to get you to part with a piece of your brownie, just say NO (nicely).

Lab-Mix GINGER and Chocolate Lab MAX
don't need caffeine to wake them up—
just a quick dip in the pool
(Max dives in, Ginger just dips her paws).

Save the "Hide"

Tip 29: Whole rawhides can hurt my stomach.

Did you know that rawhides could be hazardous to my health? I might break off sharp pieces and swallow them and, since rawhide doesn't break down in my stomach, it could irritate my digestive tract. • If your dog really likes rawhide, make sure any chew toy you give him is made from compressed rawhide. Otherwise, try a boiled bone or a bully stick (don't go for the pig ears—they're just as hazardous as rawhide). Also, if you do give me rawhide, get me the one made in the US (the South American stuff is very salty and has lots of chemicals in it).

photo: A. & J. Reinhart

Pound-rescue pup SALLY loves her chew toys so much, she walks her mom and dad right over to the pet store —no matter where they're supposed to be going!

Random Vet Visit

Tip 30: I would like the vet more if every time I went he didn't do weird things to me.

Do you like going to the doctor, where you're poked and prodded and people stick things in you? Yeah, and you know *why* it's happening. We don't. That's why every now and then it's a good idea to take me to the vet to "get weighed". No, I'm not fat. "Getting weighed" is code for "going to the hospital when everything is fine, so I don't equate the vet with only horrible things and being sick." Call the vet and see if it's okay to swing by sometime just to say "hi". You'll be amazed at how much easier it will make our next visit.

photo: C. Schelling

Samoyed RIPLEY loves her vet
—after all, that's where she goes to get fluffed!

How about we swing by the vet's for a cookie?

Living With Dogs: Chez Hanson

"How about some dog food?" • At first, I wasn't sure Polly Hanson was talking to me. • "I just made some dinner for Smedley and Little Bear. Want some?" • Yup, she was talking to me. • As I fol-lowed her into the kitchen, the two dogs padded behind, overtaking me and finally cutting me off in their haste to get to the stove, where Polly was spooning something that looked a lot like porridge into three bowls—one for me. • "Try it, she said," handing me a spoon. • I glanced down at Smedley and Little Bear, who needed no such urging, and scooped up a taste. • Polly couldn't help but laugh at the expression on my face as I tried to identify the complex, and delicious, combination of ingredients I'd tasted.

• "... Almonds ... chicken, and potato, and—are those lentils?" • "Yes. What else?" • This was amazing. "Okay, carrots definitely. And, I think those are currants, but I can't figure out what's giving it the texture. Is it the potato gluten?" • "There's Cream of Wheat in there. And some pasta, and pumpkin, and

seven-grain cereal." Polly looks down at her dogs, licking their bowls clean. "It's a meal no human being with a lick of sense would turn away or send back."
• Darned if she wasn't right. I wanted to take some home with me, but I didn't think Smedley would let me. • Polly reaches down and rubs Smedley's ears.

"He's allergic to beef," she says of her oldest dog, a long-time, much-loved visitor at various health care facilities. "It happened about ten years ago, he just started getting hives after eating. We were doing volunteer work at a mental health center at the time, and the people at the hospital suggested I stop giving him store-bought food and switch to people food. I did, and he's been fine ever since." • Polly urges her clients to make their dogs less reliant on dog food products, explaining that a varied diet of fresh food prevents a dog from getting deficient in the variety of bacterial flora that aid in digestion. "Give a dog one kind of food, one made with by-products, and that dog will only be able to process one specific kind of food," Polly explains. "It's simply healthier for dogs to eat naturally." • If only *my* cooking tasted so good!

Tribute to a Dog

Arguably one of the greatest speeches of all time, these words were spoken in 1870 by Senator Gordon Vest of Missouri, at the trial of a man accused of shooting another man's dog.

"Gentlemen of the jury: The best friend a man has in the world may turn against him and become his enemy. His son or daughter that he has reared with loving care may prove ungrateful. Those who are nearest and dearest to us, those whom we trust with our happiness and our good name may become traitors to their faith. The money that a man has, he may lose. It flies away from him, perhaps, when he needs it most. A man's reputation may be sacrificed in a moment of ill-considered action. The people who are prone to fall on their knees to do us honor when success is with us may be the first to throw the stone of malice when failure settles its clouds upon our heads. • "The one absolutely unselfish friend that many can have in this selfish world, the one that never deserts him, the one that never proves ungrateful or treacherous, is his dog. A man's dog stands by him in prosperity and poverty, in health and sickness. He will sleep on the ground, where the wintry winds blow and the snow drives fiercely, if only he may be near his master's side. He will kiss the hand that has no food to offer; he will lick the wounds and sores that come in encounter with the roughness of the world. He guards the sleep of his pauper master as if he were a prince. When all other friends desert, he remains. When the riches take wings and reputation falls to pieces, he is constant in his love as the sun in its journey through the heavens. • "If fortune drives the master forth an outcast in the world, friendless and homeless, the faithful dog asks no higher privilege than that of accompanying him, to guard against danger, to fight against his enemies, and when the last scene of all comes, and death takes the master in his embrace, and his body is lain away in the cold ground, no matter if all other friends pursue their way, there by the graveside will the noble dog be found, his head between his paws, his eyes sad, but open in alert watchfulness, faithful and true even in death." • *The plaintiff won his case.*

When three-year old Emma
was asked in school to make her family tree,
she placed her dog ALICE at the very heart.

Toenail Clipping Can Be Fun

Tip 31: Use dummy clippers when you play with me sometimes and I won't get scared when you really trim my nails.

s claw clipping a problem in your house? It was in mine — until my dad did something really neat. He bought a set of round clippers and removed the sharp blade. Then, while we were cuddling and he was massaging my toes and brushing me, he got out the "dummy" clippers and

Ready for my "peticure"!

"cut" my claws. Now I've gotten so used to having someone messing around with my toes, I get less scared when he goes at my claws with the real thing. I sometimes can't even tell which is which!

photo: E. Sanchez

ELLA is a Yellow Lab who loves being groomed,
especially with her shedding brush.
It helps her look her best
when she's riding her skateboard—
which she does beautifully!

When Something "Clicks"

Tip 32: A clicker is a great way to tell me I've done something good.

Have you ever heard of "clickers"? Little hand-held snapping instruments that make this "click" sound? You can find them in pet catalogues and some pet stores, and they're great for telling me when I've made you happy. The second, I mean the very SECOND, I do something you like, just click the clicker and give me a treat. That click helps me "imprint" the moment in my mind. With repetition, I'll figure out that you like it when I don't lunge at an unfamiliar dog, or when I let the baby play with my ears.

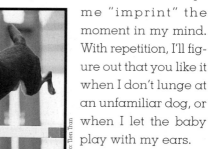

photo: Tien Tran

Mixed-breed GRIPPER went from "unreachable" by humans to an agility title-holder— thanks to love and "clicker" training.

Wow! Did I just do
something great?
What the heck was it?
Can you tell me?!
Quick, tell me,
I want to do it again!

911 For Dogs

Tip 33: Remember this number—
The National Animal Poison Control Center, 1-800-345-4735.

Have my legs suddenly stopped working, even though I haven't been in any accident you've seen? Do you have macadamia nuts in the house? Did you know that these nuts are toxic to me, and must be kept out of my reach? • There are lots of things in the house that you may not realize are harmful, even fatal, to us dogs—which is why it's a good idea to keep the number of the National Animal Poison Control Center by your phone. • By the way, they also have a web site: http://www. napc. aspca.org

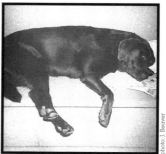

photo: J. Beaver

ALEXANDRA is known as
the "Crater Creator" at her house
—put her ball on the ground outside, and
...well, you can guess what happens next.

Let It Snow

Tip 34: A little petroleum jelly on my paws will protect me from the snow.

Not all of us dream of pulling a sled. Some of us don't even like cold sidewalks. But did you know that snow—and snow melting compounds—can irritate my paws? I might not be able to tell you, but they do. In extreme cases you might see me hop around while I'm outside, usually from the salt in the snow, which stings. • Before taking me out in the snow, rub a little petro-

leum jelly into my paws. Better yet (if I'm game) try those winter booties you used to laugh at when you saw them on your neighbor's puppy! (Did you also know that I might lick those harmful chemicals and salts off my paws and ingest them? Make sure you keep a pan of clean water by the front door during the winter months, to wash my paws in when I'm coming back inside. That'll keep me on my toes!)

photo: D. Fired, S. Oppenheim

Rescued Border-Collie MOWE (rhymes with Joey)
loves her off-leash time in the park—
any time of year. She's small for her breed
(only twenty-five pounds),
but that doesn't start her from
herding the Rottweilers and Shepherds
she plays with.

Freeze!

Tip 35: Steer clear of antifreeze!

It's one of the more lethal substances to me. Even a trace amount of antifreeze can send me into kidney failure. While the sweet-tasting ethylene glycol in antifreeze may be tempting to me, it breaks down into a compound that is highly toxic to my nervous system. Purchasing pet-safe antifreeze for your car is a good start. But even more danger-

ous to me than our car are the green puddles that build up on the street where cars park. Keep me away! • (And watch for signs of poisoning: vomiting, lethargy, or signs of intoxication similar to those from alcohol, as well as depression and diminishing urinary output.)

photo: G. & M. McCormack

Cocker Spaniel DR. WATSON loves winter,
and not for the antifreeze!
Winter is when he appears
in his local Christmas pageant
—as a Sheepdog.

The Biggest Heart: Prospect Part 2—Making Friends, Looking for Home

It turned out Prospect was about a year old, an unspayed and relatively healthy girl. During her first three days at the hospital, she voided herself of rice and beans, fried chicken parts, and paper she'd either been fed or had rooted out of the Brooklyn trash. I visited her every day, and marveled at how gentle she was, curling her body into my lap, letting the doctors examine her without incident or even a glance of complaint to me. The staff loved her, but everyone wondered if her gentle demeanor was mere weakness, and what kind of dog she would be once she got her strength back. • As soon as she was healthy enough, we moved her into the basement kennel. The hospital was expensive, and I knew I was racking up quite a bill. As her temporary owner, I had to assess her before I could in good conscience adopt her out. That meant pinching my pennies—and moving Prospect downstairs. • Over the next several weeks, Prospect got bigger —and stronger. She was a jumper, an enthusiastic dog who just didn't know her own strength. She loved everyone but, boy, could she knock you on your behind. It was as if she was making up for her tethered past with a year's worth of pent-up energy. • Every night I would get in her cage with her and go through a ritual that pleased her no end. I would bring her a special treat and then I would give her a massage. It didn't matter what kind of treat I brought, sometimes it was a few pieces of baloney, or a piece of fruit, or a meatball from the pizza place down the street. Sometimes it was a toy for her to work her jaws out on, or a bully stick, which was her favorite thing in the world.

Sometimes I'd just bring her a fresh bowl of kibble. The treat was secondary to the time we spent together and the giving of love, the gift that meant so much to her. Soon I would come down to the kennel late at night only to find her awake, sitting at attention, awaiting our visit. ● She also awaited her massage. I would start with her ears, then her neck and shoulders, at which point she would lie on her back and push her belly toward me. I would rub her belly, then work on her legs, right down to her toes. She loved it, snuffling with contentment as I eased away all the tension of her confinement, if only for a short while. ● Other strays would come. Other strays would go. People would consider Prospect, and twice she was even adopted. But she was returned, by people who cried as they handed her back. They had seen her heart, but were simply unable to deal with her energy. • As time went by and Prospect and I grew closer, I began to fear that she would never find a home. Holidays were tough in that kennel with my girl, but even as I grew financially strapped and emotionally wrecked, Prospect never lost hope, never wavered. She began to calm down too, growing up in what she now seemed to regard as her home. • The staff reached out to the Pit in the kennel too, and it seemed everyone was looking for a home for the funny pup with the wrinkly brow. We knew that whoever finally adopted her would get one of the greats, a dog that touched people with quiet dignity and a heart that wouldn't quit. • If only she had a chance. • If only she could have a chance.

4 and a Tail's Toys That Rule!

Treats aren't the only thing Sam sells. He's also seen thousands of toys leave his store clamped in the  jaws of happy dogs. Here are some of the most popular and durable toys, in no particular order:

1. **Booda Bones**: "The best, every size, every shape."
2. **Kongs**: "They can play with these for hours."
3. **Velvets**: "The bones and chips are both good. They really like the peanut butter and carrot flavors."
4. **Gum Rubber Toys [Rough and Rugged]**: "They say they're made of indestructible gum rubber, and they really are tough. Of course, there will always be a dog that can bite through anything!"
5. **Training Ball [VIP]**: "These are really good for the little dogs, especially—they keep moving!"
6. **Floppy Disc**: "Great exercise!"
7. **Doggy Hoots [any kind, any shape]**: "These are very sturdy doll toys—they're very well made. They last."
8. **Migrators**: "These duck-shaped stuffed toys are really fun—they're very popular with the bigger dogs. They really think they're ducks!"
9. **Balls**: "They'll always be popular—the higher they bounce, the better for the dog!"
10. **You**: "The best toy there is!"

Challenges

Tip 36: We love puzzle toys — especially when there are treats involved.

Here's a fun present for a rainy day, or for dogs that are big on chewing: Get one of my bones or a rubber Kong, and fill it with peanut butter. I'll spend hours just try-ing to get it all out! If you find that I really like this one, you might want to invest in one of those toys that

photo: B. Corrigan, B. Sheehan

dispense treats. They're great for when you have to leave me alone for extended periods of time!

Irish Terrier AGNES has a backyard full of toys, chew balls, rawhide, and balls—
and there's not a squirrel to be found!

The Prong Way

Tip 37: Pronged collars can be good training tools if used carefully and correctly.

Ah, the pronged collar debate! Some people believe the pronged collar is a cruel way to keep me on a leash, and I agree—if you keep me in a pronged collar, that is. The way I see it, when we're being trained, some of us big guys don't know our own strength. We don't really know that we're pulling you around, especially when we get distracted. That prong collar tells us that we're tugging and helps us learn to heel. If used properly, the pronged collar will serve as "training wheels" in a big dog's leash training, and will only be necessary for "tune-ups" after a while. So take it from a big guy:

- Treat the prong collar as a teaching tool, not a permanent walking collar.
- Use it as a last resort, not a first step.

Don't bother me,
I'm training.

- Make sure the collar you choose for me is the right size (your veterinarian can help you with this).
- Make sure you've tried the Gentle Leader Headcollar. It's designed to apply pressure not to our throats but to the back of our necks, which instinctively makes us relax. It comes very highly recommended—check out their web site (www.gentle leader.com).

photo: B. Bauman

Malamute/Red Husky-mix SKYE
prefers an elegant leather leash—
it looks great on her!

Fetch Me Something New!

Tip 38: Sticks are always fun, especially when you get creative with them.

The next time you toss me a stick, think about tossing one of these:

- A Brussels sprout stalk—they're delicious, tough, and good for me.

- Sugar cane—what a special treat... I'll wonder what I've done to get such a present!

- A carrot stick—they're not just for rabbits anymore!

photo: G. Statti

Yorkie THEODORE is a huge carrot fan (baby carrots, please!), but he won't say no to broccoli, freeze-dried liver treats—and maybe a candy cane or two.

By the time he gets to
Little League, he's gonna be
something, boy!

Commands

Tip 39: Learning basic commands is necessary before successful socializing.

There are so many things I will learn from socializing, but there are several commands I MUST know BEFORE you take me to a park or let me go off with my buddies:

"COME!"
(Or whatever word you choose for "Get back here!")

"DOWN!"
(Sometimes I need to hear this command to help ward off aggressors)

"TREAT!" or **"LOOK AT ME!"**
(Or my own name—whatever will get me to look at you and turn away from something—or someone—I shouldn't be focusing on)

Please… I know they sound obvious, but my knowing these commands is for the good of every dog in the pack. If you can't get me to obey these commands easily, other dogs will see and hear your stress (and so will their owners), and they might not respond in a way any of us would like.

photo: D. Charvez

ATTICUS is a beautiful Border Collie
who let's his mom know how grateful he is
that she rescued him with every sigh!

That Time of the Month

Luckily, my owner loves me enough to have me spayed but, believe me, they don't call it "heat" for nothing. A girl who hasn't been spayed can go through hell. At least once a year, the intact female runs the risk of taking off in search of relief, and if she comes back, you can end up with a whole litle of little pups in need of responsible care. She also runs a higher risk of breast cancer than a spayed dog. • Spaying your

Bring me a MAAAN!

female means she won't get uterine cancer, ovarian cancer, or pyometritis, an infection in the uterus that can prove fatal. And don't believe the myth about how "going through one heat cycle is good for her health"—getting your female dog altered at about six months of age is a great way of helping keep her healthy. That way, she can focus on the people she already loves—for a long time to come.

photo: S. Caruso

She was found running wild in a Baltimore park
when she was two years old,
but Doberman Pinscher JADE is gentle and dainty
and much more suited to the loving home
she's been living in ever since.

Living with Dogs: Labels for Everything

"Tommy has this *enormous* bark."
• Trainer Polly Hanson is sitting on the floor of her kitchen. Tommy, the Rottweiler she and her husband, Bud Greenberg, are fostering, is asleep, his head in Polly's lap. Tommy is missing an ear, a grim reminder of the abuse he's suffered in his young life. Yet, under Polly and Bud's loving guidance, Tommy has thrived, cohabiting with the three other dogs in the household.• "I want people to like my dogs," Polly is known to say, and one can imagine how difficult that could be with big ol' Tommy. "That's why we worked out a game when it comes to his bark. He can't change the way he barks, but I can give his bark a label so that it becomes a com-

photos: P. Hanson, B. Greenberg

mand, something that can work in his favor. • "I gave the 'bark' command a name that will help people who don't know him—'*whisper*.' Now, when we're walking or out in the park and we see someone new I'll say, 'Tommy—*whisper*.' Then he lets out this huge 'A-WOOF!'" She laughs, as Tommy stirs in his sleep. "I'll say to the new person, 'Imagine what he sounds like when he's not whispering!'—That usually helps the other person relax." • Polly and Bud give labels to all of the things their dogs do, and they instruct the owners of the dogs they train to do the same. The labels they choose are always

photos: P. Hanson, B. Greenberg

designed for society, for the people their dogs come in contact with, and not so much for the dogs themselves. • Later, when the dogs are on their walk, Polly gives another example. She points to Little Bear, her Chow. "When he came to us," Polly says, "no one could put a collar on him. It was only after gaining his trust that we found the cigarette burns on Little Bear's neck and realized that a collar and leash had been instrumental in torturing him." • It's hard to believe that the dog walking patiently at

Polly's side was ever abused so terribly. Especially when he sees someone walking up the street with a Sheltie in tow. • "Little Bear, *look*! A *friend, a friend! Go say hello!*" As Little Bear trots up to the dog, both tails start wagging. Polly says to the owner, "Little Bear *loves* making friends. He's *very* gentle." • If the Sheltie owner was at all anxious about the Chow and the reputation of the breed, his fears abate when his dog sniffs Little Bear, hopping into playing stance. The Sheltie barks, pulling his leash to get closer, but Little Bear remains silent, tail wagging, but ready to resume his walk. • "Dogs are hard-wired to sniff each other out," Polly explains. "They identify each other that way, it's instinctive. But in the world that Little Bear—that all big dogs—live in, it's important that people not be afraid of them as they go about their business. So the words I choose for Little Bears' sniffing other dogs aren't *'Don't be afraid, he won't hurt you, he's just sniffing you dog'*, but *'A friend, a friend, go say hello'* so people will like him. • "These words are usually enough to make other people relax. If they're still nervous, we just move on." Polly smiles. "The dogs are always happy to keep walking. They love their walks so much." • It may appear that Polly Hanson is not so much training dogs as she is training society, that she's saying to other humans, "Don't be afraid of a dog for simply being a dog." • What Polly is really doing is teaching both species to coexist, and appreciate what is best in each other.

photos: P. Hanson, B. Greenberg

A Dream Come True:
Clive Barker

For 25 years, Clive Barker has dazzled us with his plays, novels, short stories, screenplays, directing and painting, all of which seem to only scratch at the surface of one of today's most visionary artists. A true master of fantasy and horror, one only has to read one of his stories or watch one of his films to know that Clive takes dreams very seriously. • *It therefore comes as no surprise to learn how his beloved canine family suddenly grew in number a few years back...*

At the time, there were three dogs living in the Los Angeles house. Lola, the *grande dame* German shepherd, her son, Ubu and Spaniel-mix Bart, the irascible old man of the bunch, who had joined the family when David Armstrong, Clive's partner, moved

Photo of, from left to right, Ubu, Jason Bartholemew
Armstrong Barker"Bart" , Lola, Macy, Charlie and Clive

in. • "It was David who woke up one morning and out of the blue told me, 'There's a dog waiting for us somewhere,'" Clive said. "Just like that." Never one to take dreams lightly and not about to start doing so, Clive and David set out for their local dog pound. • It was a shepherd-mix with somber eyes that turned out to be 'waiting' for them. "Charlie spoke to us loudly," Clive recalls, and they adopted the dog on the spot. But as it turned out, fate wasn't quite finished with them. • "While I was filling out the forms on Charlie, someone told David about this 'last-ditch' deal for dogs over in Pasadena that was happening the following Sunday. Apparently, these people out there were going to set up a sort of adoption site for all these dogs who had exhausted their shelter possibilities and were on their way to… well, *on their way*." Ever the animal lover, David volunteered to help and the following Sunday, both David and Clive headed to Pasadena. • That was where they found a year-old black-and-tan mix that clung to Clive. "He was a mess," Clive remembers of his first meeting with Macy. "He had a bum leg, wounds all over him, and this tumor under his tongue that made it hard for him to eat. And there he was, saying to me 'I'm your dog.'" • They adopted Macy without hesitation and took him home, where they set about getting the dog's tumor removed and his injuries tended to. It would take a long time for Macy to recover, but his spirit would never lag. The rescued puppy found his place in

the Barker/Armstrong pack immediately—wherever Clive was. •
It seemed like the happiest of endings—but one thing continued to puzzle Clive. "How did we end up with *two* dogs, when David had been so certain in his dream that there was *one* dog out there waiting for us?" Clive couldn't help but wonder what it meant that there were two new faces in their bunch as a result of David's vision. • The answer proved a difficult one to deal with. It wasn't until Macy was finally on the mend that Charlie started to get sick. It was back to the vet, with another dog—but this time the prognosis was terrifying. Charlie had disptemper, and the happy ending had suddenly become a potential nightmare. The highly communicable virus was more than a threat to poor Charlie—it put the lives of all the other dogs at serious risk. •

In the end Lola, Ubu, Bart and Macy didn't get sick, something Clive can only describe as a "miracle", and while Charlie died soon after he was diagnosed, he died in the arms of people who had loved him, if only for a brief time. • And so the meaning behind the dream of the waiting dog was revealed, to Clive, who's philosophical about the happy ending. • "I like to think that David and I were sent to Charlie because we could give him comfort and love in the little time he had left. And we were sent to Macy because he was waiting to begin a new life with us." • He's certainly made a dent there. Quick to glue himself to Clive's side or try a new trick, Macy has proven to be a most loyal and loving addition to the house where love is in abundance—and dreams come true.

Ticked Off

L ots of people try and remove ticks with blown-out matches, burning the tick with the hot match head. This can REALLY BACKFIRE, guys! People also panic if they don't get the entire tick out. • The best way to remove a tick is with a tool specifically designed for the purpose (you can get it at your pet store), or with

a pair of tweezers. If you don't get the whole tick out, don't worry. I may scratch at it a bit, but I'll be okay. Just use a little Betadine or antiseptic on the area to prevent a hot spot. And remember, ticks can carry diseases that are communicable to humans, so wash your hands thoroughly if you touch that tick!

photo: E. Barrows

No ticks on HORATIO!
This Cocker Spaniel is the picture of health,
and he should be—
his mom is a Veterinary Assistant.

Hotel Le Paws

Tip 42: Choose my kennel carefully, and help make it feel like home.

Taking a trip? Am I staying in a hotel, too? It can feel like a vacation for me too, you know, if you help make my kennel experience a pleasant one.
• Make sure the boarding facility you choose for me has a dog run and/or team of good dog-walkers who will give me lots of quality time.

Be sure to leave me with a few of my favorite toys (label them!), as well as things that smell like you (a blanket, a shirt, or a towel you've used), so I won't miss you so much. Check and see if the brand of kibble I like is the kind the kennel uses (if it isn't, leave my brand); if I'm a "people-food" eater, arrange for a

friend to come in with my prepared meal to drop off. ● And while we're on those "friends" of yours, get a few people I know to drop in and visit me (be sure to make all appropriate arrangements with the kennel before you go). Before any of us know it, you'll be back home —and I'll be ready for the next time!

Standard Poodle BENNY will go anywhere
—so long as his brother is nearby.

Adopt Me

Tip 43: Pure breeds need rescuing, too!

Thinking of getting a new Newfie? • Know someone who wants a pure Peke? • Did you know that the American Kennel Club has a web site devoted to each recognized breed, where people post listings for dogs of all ages that have been displaced or are in need of adoption? You can help save the life of a dog already in need of your love. • Just visit the AKC website: http://www.akc.org

photo: D. Herman

Chihuahua PI was adopted from the San Francisco SPCA, and everyone who meets her agrees she is one of the more striking dogs they've ever seen!

What's for Dinner?

Tip 44: The primary ingredient in my food should be meat.

Did you know that I might be allergic to grain? My digestive system might have difficulty accepting the amount of grain you find in some brands of commercial dog food. If my diet contains kibble and canned food, make sure the main ingredient is MEAT. And I don't mean "meat by-products." (By-products are the parts of animals that are deemed unfit for human consumption, and "digest of by-product" is...well, you don't want to know). So bypass the by-product—and bring on the beef!

photo: C. Kies

Husky BEAR loves his meat—
almost as much as he loves taking a nap after eating!

Time to Say Goodbye

You've always said I tell you everything. • You've always said I talk to you and let you know what I'm thinking. • Well, there's one thing I'll never say. I will never tell you that I want to go. I will never tell you that it's time to say goodbye. • Not until you tell me it's okay. • And someday, I may need you to tell me that. I know you will, because

I'll always be there
for you, too.

there's no one in the world who loves me more. And there's no one in the world that loves you more. •
I don't want you to hurt. I need to know that you're okay. I need to know that more than anything. •
And then everything will be fine. I believe that. You should, too.

Tibetan Terrier GEOFFREY
lived to be fifteen.
He will always be both missed and loved.

"Open Vessels": The Educated Puppy

photo: courtesy P. Hanson, B. Greenberg

Barbara Giella is a new puppy-owner's second-best friend—a position she has taken seriously for over fifteen years. • Back then Giella, a college professor with a doctorate in art history, became a puppy-owner for the second time. "I had an overwhelming desire to learn how to raise Abby, to understand what she needed most." Living in a city, Giella discovered that many urban puppies weren't receiving formal training until long after they got their booster shots. "These puppies were very under-socialized. A six-week-old puppy is in a critical socialization period—this is the best time for a puppy to begin systematically learning how to live with humans. Yet socialization at two and three months appeared to be a suburban phenomenon. City puppies just weren't starting their training early enough." • Giella was also surprised at the lack of support available to puppy-owners. "There can be such a feeling of helplessness in some owners," she says. They feel as if they have no control over their dogs, that they can't understand them. Someone had to help these people interpret their puppies' behaviors, and understand that they had more control than they thought." • Enter The Educated

Puppy, Giella's school for puppies and their owners. Together with her team of volunteers, Giella offers group classes, one-on-one coaching and even home visits for the entire family of the new four-legged friend. • "Whether or not you choose to train your puppy early, he or she is inevitably learning from every experience and every interaction," Giella says about her program. "I urge my clients to take an active role in their puppy's education." • If Giella's method sounds like that of the successful rearing of a child—it is, in a way. "Puppies, like children, should not be allowed to simply 'hang out', supervised or not. They should be moved from activity to activity, including naps, chew-time, training sessions, and exercise outdoors if they're old enough." • And if they're too young to go outside? "Your puppy should be exercised thoroughly on a regular basis. Besides good nutrition, it is the single most important strategy in raising a well mannered pup. Exercising the pup while she is in quarantine awaiting the completion of her shots can be challenging. It is possible, however —if you do a lot of activities with your puppy, such as games or reward-based training. You can even create a little obstacle course —use your imagination." Or the puppy, Giella explains, will use hers. "Don't expect the little dear to simply not bother you for attention and then get angry or frustrated when she occupies herself excavating your couch or tries to get your attention by chewing on you as she would another pup." • When it comes to chewing, Giella proves an excellent teacher—for humans. "One of the most common mistakes new puppy owners make is to inadvertently reward their pups for undesirable behavior. They wait until the pup is chewing on the couch then give him a bone to chew instead. It's far more effective to find the chewies the puppy adores—and this can take some time—and offer them *before* the chewing and nipping occurs." This may not work for a puppy whose social or exercise needs have not been met, which proves further that puppies are so much more than just cute little balls of fur. • It's hard to believe that a six-week-old puppy is ready to tackle such behaviors as chewing and nipping, peeing or pooping in the wrong place, and barking. But as Giella has demonstrated for years, puppies are not only ready to learn—an 'Educated Puppy' grows up to be a remarkable dog.

Giella is a member of the Association of Pet Dog Trainers and is recomended by the ASPCA. There are puppy trainers all over the country able to get you and your dog-in-waiting ready for life together. Ask your vet for a list of qualified names!

Visit the Educated Puppy & Dogs, Too
at www.educatedpuppy.com

The Biggest Heart: Prospect
Part 3—After

Warning: there is no happy ending to the story of Prospect. But there is a real story, just like one that is unfolding somewhere else, with another dog, right now. I tell this story not to break your heart, but to give her life purpose beyond my memory of her—and to try and make a difference in another dog's life, a dog I'll never know, somewhere I'll never be.

Prospect died. • She died nine months after I found her in the park, and a month after being adopted by one of the technicians at the hospital where she had boarded for so long. He had trained her to follow commands and walk on a leash beautifully. She loved her new owner, probably more than she loved me. She adored the two other dogs she shared her new home with—and they adored her. • Prospect was fed one day by someone who didn't understand how protective the dogs could be when it came to their food. A fight ensued, and Prospect was bitten. She stayed in hospital for three days, where they nursed her injuries until her heart, that big, wonderful heart, finally gave out. My last memory of her is of her rolling over on her back in the hospital, her tail thapping in anticipation of a belly rub. I rubbed her belly that night, for a long time. I never saw her again. • Over those three days I saw people at the hospital whom I'd never met, but who knew Prospect, and loved her. I never realized how many people had fallen for my girl and tried to help her during her long search for a home. • Time has passed, and I don't blame anyone for Prospect's death. I don't blame the people who abandoned her, or myself for taking her in. I don't blame the owner, or the dog that bit her or the person who gave them the food that caused the fight. Those final weeks at home were joyful ones, probably the only really joyful time she had ever known, and while her end was tragic, I believe that Prospect was here for a reason. I celebrate her love, a love that she offered unselfishly to the very end. • Was she expensive? Yes. Did she break my heart? Yes. • Was she supposed to have died that day in the park when I first found her? Did I intervene on some cosmic plane and give her time she wasn't supposed to have? I actually asked myself questions like that, because her end seemed so senseless. Then I realized that Prospect's end was senseless only if it truly was an end. • So I tell her story. And we all miss her, a big dog with a heart to match. And the next time we see a dog, we remember her. • Would I do it again? Would I take in another skinny stranger? • I would—and I will. • For Prospect.

Not Just Bad for the Breath

Tip 46: Onions are bad for me.

Okay, so you can't resist and you're going to give him a piece of that hamburger. It's meat, right? Good for him, right? • Let him have it—but HOLD THE ONIONS. Onions can potentially damage red blood cells and cause hemolytic anemia. That's right. Onions. Cooked, uncooked, doesn't matter. Onions (and garlic, by the way) are a big no-no in a dog's diet so, next time you toss him a meatball, make sure that you know what's in it won't hurt him.

photo: courtesy J. Thaler

When he's not playing tug-of war with his family, Wheaton Terrier FERGUS is chewing the faces off all the toys in the house.

No thanks,
I've got too many
people to kiss.

Soft Mouths

Tip 47: Biting is necessary—controlling biting is the key!

Fact: Dogs bite. • Fact: Dogs NEED TO BITE. It's what we're meant to do. • Fact: You can't stop me from biting—but you can stop me from biting what you don't want me to, and you CAN stop me from biting hard. • The secret is giving me lots of toys to chew and bite—this lets me work out my biting instincts on things that have been approved by you. And let me know when my mouthing gets too tough. This will teach me to CONTROL the pressure of my biting, help me develop a "soft mouth" and keep all of us happy!

photo: Rick Reason, courtesy D. Seltzer

With her strong maternal instincts, nine-year old mixed breed BEE BEE is known as the "Hall Monitor" of her neighborhood park. She protects the little dogs, and rescues them from rough play— when she's not chasing squirrels or swimming, that is.

Oops.
Sorry about that.

Cool Down!

Tip 48: Ice is a great way to cool down our body temperature fast.

Here's a great treat for a hot summer day: Get a plastic container and fill it with water, then freeze it (leave the top off). When I'm just lying around wishing it was snowing, give me my "frozen water bowl" to lick. This is also a great thing to take to the park, or for after play (once I've cooled down a bit). And it will keep those trips to the flushing water fountain down, too (Boy, that toilet keeps the water nice and cold)!

photo: courtesy D. Gillman

CHAUCER is a Soft-Coated Wheaten Terrier who loves it outside— that's where he herds all his friends!

Sniffing to Know You

Tip 49: Smelling people is my way of shaking hands. Please let me go first!

Want to alleviate some of my anxiety? • I know how good-looking I am, and I know all of your friends are nice. But I'd really like to get a good whiff of them before they go reaching to hug me and stuff. My nose tells me who they are a lot better than my eyes

do. So could you tell your friends and family to let me walk up to them and smell them first? If they hold out their hands to me, palm down, fingers in (like a closed paw) I'll be thrilled—and ready to play in no time at all. • Thanks. Knew I could count on you!

Jack Russell BETTER knows what the mailman smells like— here's how he's found out!

photo: L. Zuzzi

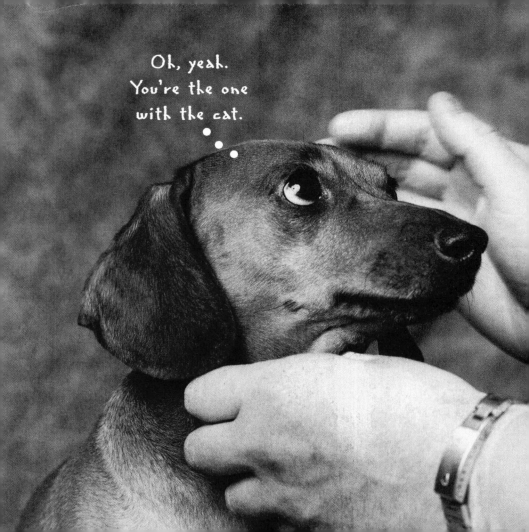

Best Friends—For Life

Tip 50: We are all unique, and wonderful to know.

So did you know we knew so much? • Good for you. But let me remind you of another thing you probably know. • No two dogs are alike. We are all magnificent, possessing individual gifts, with different likes, dislikes, fears, hopes, and ways of communicating. • What's good for one of us may be unpleasant for another. You're the best judge of who your dog is and what your dog is saying to you. • Enjoy your time together. See you around!

photo: Nancy DeJesus

COCOA is a Chihuahua who loves to cuddle in mom's large slippers. He loves to run and play fetch with his green tennis ball.

What You Can Do to Help

Want to reach out to the dogs of the world? Here are some ways you can help do it!

Adopt!
Go to the shelters, go to the pound. Be sensible, and save a life.

Volunteer!
The shelters need good volunteers to walk the dogs, clean their living areas and give them love. Remember: the more contact a stray dog has with people, the more open she will be to being approached by that person who is meant to take her home!

Open your wallet!

There are small animal rescue organizations that are in need of your financial support. Seek out your local organization and make a donation. Let them know how much their wonderful work is appreciated.

Form a neighborhood lookout!

Find out which of your neighbors have experience with dogs and/or dog rescue, and learn how to rescue a stray. Get your concerned neighbors to keep a 'rescue pack' in their homes—with a slip on leash, an easy-open can of dog food, a pack of treats, a bottle of water, a water bowl and the numbers of other neighbors who have experience and room for an overnight visitor. Put together a fund for your lookout group so that these dogs can be boarded while you look for a home.

Reach out to dog-owners!

If you see a dog-owner having difficulty with a new dog, be kind. So many people 'give up' on their dogs because they feel alone out there and frustrated and embarrassed with the behaviors they're trying to work out. Talk to these people. Volunteer the name of a good trainer, or volunteer your dog for an introduction or even a play date. Share you experiences with others, and let them share their experiences with you. You may help a relationship survive!

Love the dog you're with!

Train your dog, keep your dog healthy, keep your dog stimulated, make sure your dog has all his shots and identification, and most of all…

Listen to what your dog is saying!